Read · Think · Do

MATH

Ages 6 & Up

Adding and Subtracting Book 2

Ann Montague-Smith

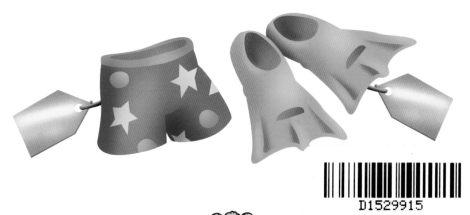

Teacher Created Resources

Copyright © QEB Publishing 2005

First published in the United States by
QEB Publishing, Inc.
23062 La Cadena Drive
Laguna Hills
CA 92653

This edition published by
Teacher Created Resources, Inc.
6421 Industry Way
Westminster, CA 92683

www.teachercreated.com

Library of Congress Control Number: 2005921280

ISBN 1-4206-8177-X

Written by Ann Montague-Smith
Designed and edited by The Complete Works
Illustrated by Peter Lawson
Photography by Steve Lumb

Publisher Steve Evans
Creative Director Louise Morley
Editorial Manager Jean Coppendale

Printed and bound in China

With thanks to:

Contents

Adding small numbers

Add each set of numbers on the cars. Find that total on a driver's helmet. That's the driver of that car!

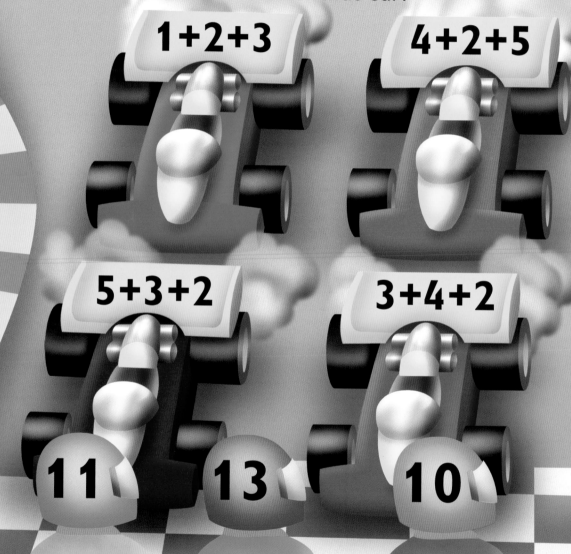

1+2+3

4+2+5

5+3+2

3+4+2

11

13

10

What happens if you add the numbers in a different order? Is the total the same or different?

4+5+3

Challenge

Use the numbers 1 to 10.
Find three numbers which make a
total of 20. Can you find 5 different
ways of doing this? Check your totals
by adding in a different order.

9+4+7=20

6+4+3

4+7+3

6   12   9   14

5

I know these

Find a friend, a coin, and two board game tokens. Take turns to throw the coin onto the spinner. Move your token forward the number your coin lands on, and answer the question on the lily pad. If you answer correctly, leave your token there. If you are wrong, move back to where you were. The winner is the first one to the finish.

Start

5+4

3+6

50+50

4+2

5+3

30+70

8–3

7–2

5+5

5–3

8–7

10–10

100–80

4+6

10+90

spinner

1 2
4 3

Now try this

Take three of these numbers: 1, 2, 3, 4, 5, 6, 7. You can only choose each number once for each addition sentence you come up with. Write 4 different addition problems that total 10.

$$3+6+1=10$$

100–30

100–60

8+2

9+1

20+80

2+8

10–5

3+7

20+8

100–50

40+60

9–3

6–6

6+2

Finish

1+9

100–100

7

I know totals for 20

Get 21 board game tokens or coins. Choose two numbers from the animals that total 20. Cover your numbers with the tokens.

Find different ways to make a total of 20.
Can you cover 20 of the numbers?

Challenge

Look at the numbers on the animals. Add 2 numbers together to make a total of 30. Can you find 5 ways of doing this?

$?+?=30$

9

5 and ...

You can break numbers up into "5 and a little bit more" to make adding easier, like this: 9+7=5+4+5+2=10+4+2=10+6=16. Now you can figure out how many bones are in the dogs' bags.

Try this with a friend

Take turns to choose two of these numbers: 31, 32, 33, 34, 35.

Write an addition problem using your numbers. Write the answer.

Tell your friend how you figured out the answer.

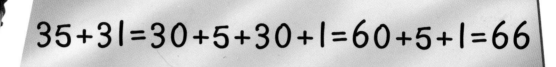

$$35+31=30+5+30+1=60+5+1=66$$

You can break tens and ones numbers up in the same way like this: 13+22=10+3+20+2=30+5=35. How many fish do the cats have in their bags?

14   25

16 13

17 27

18   21

Adding and subtracting

If you know an addition fact, then you can work out more facts like this: 16+3=19   3+16=19   19-16=3   19-3=16

16,3,19

15,8,7

18,11,7

4,19,15

20,4,16

11,5,6

Look at the numbers on the donkeys.
Find 4 different number problems for each set of numbers.

Now try this

Look at these 6 numbers:
4, 15, 7, 3, 12, 11. They are mixed up.
Can you sort the numbers into
two sets of 3? Each set of numbers
must make 4 number problems.

12,5,17

3,13,16

? + ? = ?
? + ? = ?
? − ? = ?
? − ? = ?

4,16,12

11,14,3

4,13,17

Tens and ones

Help the letter carriers figure out how many letters to put into their bags by finding the answers to the number problems on their mail bags. An easy way to work this out is to add or subtract the tens first, then do the units.

92–51

31+47

67–13

23+41

48–15

Which bag will have the most letters in it?
Which bag will have the least number of letters in it?

64+23

43+36

76−23

85−62

44+32

54−24

Try this

Choose a number from here:
20, 30, 40, 50, 60.
Now choose a number from here:
15, 17, 23, 26, 38.
Add the two numbers together.
In the answer, what do you notice
about the tens and the ones digits?
Try this 4 more times.

20+15=

15

Finding small differences

Find a butterfly with the same number difference as the orange one. Count up from the smaller to the larger number to find the difference.

62 – 55

21 – 18

24 – 19

46 – 39

52 – 48

34 – 26

Find the other pairs of butterflies with the same difference.

16

62 − 54

45 − 39

Challenge

Use two-digit numbers.
Find 5 pairs of numbers
with a difference of 6.
Write your pairs of numbers down.

64−58=6

81 − 78

61 − 57

73 − 67

51 − 46

17

Four in a row

Get some board game tokens. Choose 2 numbers from the animal statues below. Decide whether to add or find the difference between your numbers. If your answer is on the grid, cover that number with a token. Try to make a line of 4 counters from your answers.

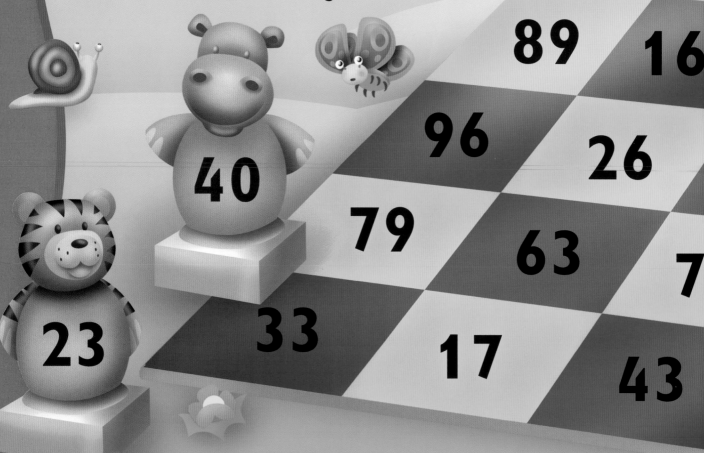

40

23

89

16

96

26

79

63

7

33

17

43

Play the game with a friend.
The first one to get 4 in a row wins!

72

36

9

10

53

13

69

49

56

19

Vacation shopping

Get some coins. Pretend to buy 2 of the things below.
Give the right amount of money when you pay.

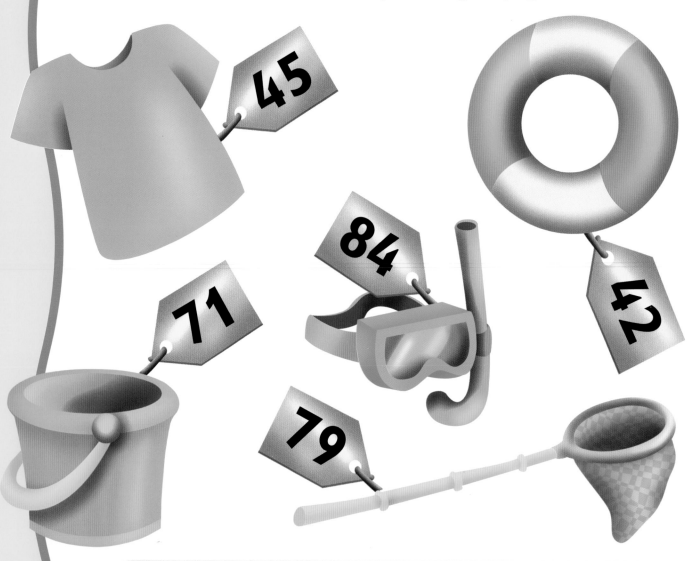

Now try this again. This time, give too much money
when you pay. Figure out the right change.

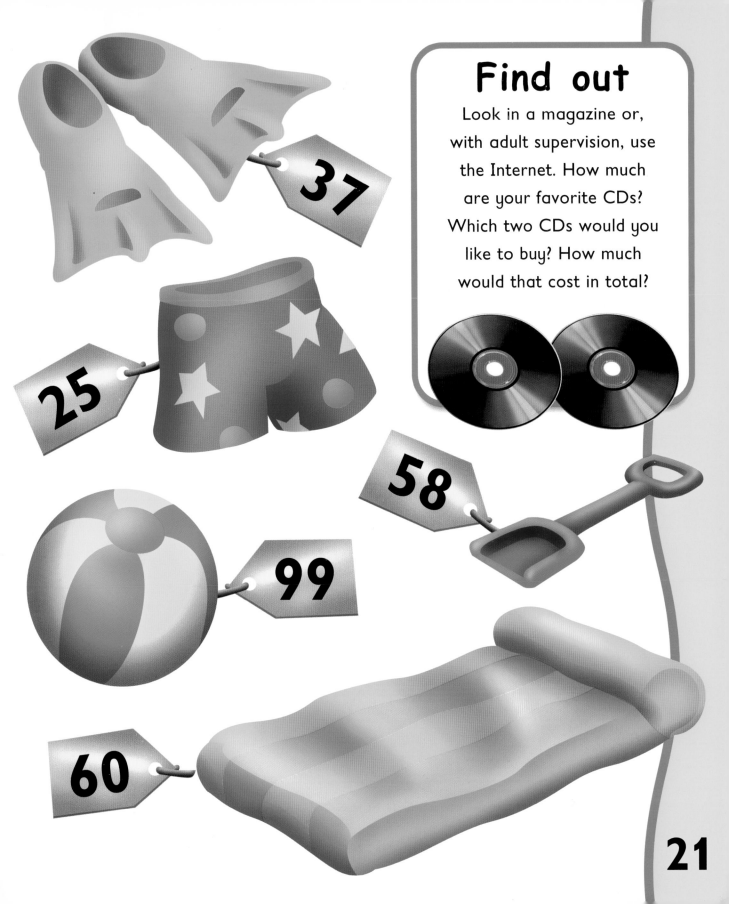

37

25

58

99

60

Find out

Look in a magazine or, with adult supervision, use the Internet. How much are your favorite CDs? Which two CDs would you like to buy? How much would that cost in total?

Supporting notes

Adding small numbers, pages 4–5

If the children need further help, there are two strategies that they might find useful: finding pairs of numbers which make 10, then adding on the third number, such as 4+7+6=4+6+7=10+7=17. Or, putting the largest number first, such as 3+5+4=5+4+3=9+3=12.

I know these, pages 6–7

Encourage the children to answer these questions as quickly as they can. These are addition and subtraction within a total of 10, and addition of multiples of 10 up to 100. If the children are unsure, remind them of strategies that they already know, such as counting up from the larger number, and using what they know about single-digit totals to 10 to find totals of multiples of 10, up to 100.

I know totals for 20, pages 8–9

Knowing totals for 20 is an extension of knowing totals for 10. For example, 2+8=10 and 12+8=20. If children are unsure, cover the tens digit and ask the children to total the units to make totals of 10, then uncover the tens digit to make a total of 20. Encourage the children to spot the pattern: 0+20=20; 1+19=20; 2+18=20…

5 and a little bit, pages 10–11

Encourage the children to work in their heads, where possible, when partitioning and recombining. If they are unsure of this, then encourage them to write addition problems which show the partitioning and recombining of the numbers.

Adding and subtracting, pages 12–13

If the children know, or can rapidly recall, one addition or subtraction fact, then they can deduce three other facts. If children are unsure about this, write down one of the facts like this: 16+3=19. Then ask, "What is 3+16? What do you notice? So what is 19-3? And 19-16? Now what do you notice?" If the children find the calculation difficult, count together using a mental number line.

Tens and units, pages 14–15

Where the addition or subtraction of the units does not cross the tens barrier, the children can use what they already know to work out the answer. They will probably find it easier to begin with the tens digits, then deal with the units. If they are unsure, use a number line and start with the tens digits.

Finding small differences, pages 16–17

Counting up from the smaller to the larger number is a useful strategy when finding small differences. If children are unsure, use a number line. Start at the smaller number and count up by ones. The children can keep track of how many are counted on their fingers. Encourage them to move to doing this in their heads.

Four in a row, pages 18–19

This game challenges the children to use addition or subtraction facts that they know, or can calculate in their heads. They may find it helpful to have paper and pencil handy when playing this game, so that they can jot down which numbers they have tried and the totals or differences.

Vacation shopping, pages 20–21

The children will find it useful to have real coins for this activity. If they find the totaling difficult, they can begin with a selection of coins and count out what they need for each price, then total the coins. Encourage them to total in their heads, then count out the coins, using the fewest coins possible.

Using this book

The illustrations in this book are bright, cheerful, and colorful, and are designed to capture children's interest. Sit somewhere comfortable together as you look at the book. Children of th[e] age will normally be able to read most of the instructional words. Help with the reading wher[e] necessary, so that all children can take part in the activities, regardless of how fluent they are reading at this point in time.

The activities in the book include recall of addition and subtraction facts for all numbers up to 10, such as 3+6; 9-1... The children use what they know about addition for a total of 10 to ma[ke] totals of 100 using multiples of 10, such as 60+40. They add and subtract tens and units, using mental methods. Encourage the children to use mental methods, such as counting up by ones to find small differences. For example, for 52-48, count up from 48 to 52: 49, 50, 51, 52. The children can keep a tally of how many they have counted on their fingers at first, and then move to doing this in their heads. Where the children are combining tens and units, they may find it helpful to make some notes on paper. One way of figuring out, for example, 36+57, is this: $36+57=30+6+50+7=80+6+7=80+13=93$.

Encourage the children to explain how they figured out the answers to the questions. Being able to explain their thinking, and to use the correct mathematical vocabulary, helps the children to clarify in their minds what they have just done. Also, for children who are not as sure of how to solve the problem, hearing what others did, and how they did it, helps them to use these methods more effectively.

Do encourage the children to make notes as they work on an activity. They can record numbers, writing them in order, or write simple sentences to explain. Encourage them to be systematic in the way that they work, so that they do not leave out a vital part of the evidence that they need to find a solution.

Above all, enjoy together the mathematical games, activities, and challenges in this book!